The Tarot Journal

of

Healing Heartbreak

BY: RED ORCHID PUBLISHING

Melanny Eva Henson

All rights reserved © Melanny Eva Henson
2020 Red Orchid Publishing

Introduction

What you hold in your hands is a piece of my heart. But I did not create this journal to showcase my heartache, but to become a collaboration of hearts. Pieces of the artist Edvard Munch's heart are featured within these pages, as are the heart fragments of several writers and philosophers. Together, we provide a platform for you to reflect and articulate. Soon, pieces of your own heart will fill these pages, and then this book will transform into something deeply personal, and (I sincerely hope) a conduit of growth and healing within your life.

Some of my wounds have taken years to heal. Often, when I give tarot readings for clients who are in a transitional phase of life, I recognize their heartbreak, their questions, and their yearnings as my own from days past. Heartbreak is a universal experience. If you live a long life, you are certain to experience it. Healing can often be so elusive. We are inundated with messages of guilt, and the overarching theme from a day's worth of internet memes will tell you that if you were confident and self-loving enough, you wouldn't be experiencing pain from heartache at all. If only, (they say) you were good enough, you wouldn't suffer. Instead of healing, we are overcome with self-doubt, which easily festers into self-loathing. Then, we are no good to anyone, least of all ourselves.

Here is the truth about healing, (and while I'm at it, here is the truth about becoming a confident and healthy person capable of overcoming exquisite heartache): no one starts out being good enough, strong enough, smart enough or wise enough. Most of us sloshed through our heartache in all its ugliness and destroyed bits of our lives in its wake. Most of us took a baseball bat and tried to batter the truth into submission. Most of us ran our pain through the wash twenty-seven times, and when we pulled it out still stained and wrinkled, we ran it through again. Most of us turned around and hurt the people still there for us. Most of us were fools. And so, dear, if you are reeling, obsessing, and withdrawing into a cocoon of self-absorbed memories, it is ok. You should know it is your job to be a fool for now, if that's all you can be, until the pain subsides with the low tide of your life.

You should befriend this foolishness and not hold yourself in contempt. Self-forgiveness is the beginning of the healing journey, and if you can't forgive yourself, then you haven't started. So give yourself permission to have shortcomings while you are learning to heal. If you're holding this book, even considering purchasing it, that means you are still picking up your pain, turning it around in your hands, and examining it. It is only the people who hide from their pain or bury it who are in real trouble in life. They refuse growth, and therefore, will not heal properly. But if you are willing to spend time with your pain, look at it again and again, change the filter, or adjust the resolution on your microscope, and look once again, you will inch closer to the person you want to be, and closer to true healing.

About Edvard Munch

I knew I wanted to create this journal for my clients before I ever connected to Edvard Munch's work. At first, I simply needed a cover image, so I looked for artists whose themes often included heartbreak. I stumbled upon Munch's piece, "Separation." The ghostly female image captured my imagination, and I was quite struck by the downtrodden man in the painting, depicted as emotionally vulnerable (a state men are rarely portrayed, in art, or elsewhere). The pain of the relationship pulsated from the canvas. I had found the perfect cover image for my journal.

My fascination with Munch's work grew. Nearly 1800 paintings by Munch exist, and a thorough evaluation of his various artistic phases reveal an illustrator competent in technique. His style and form shifts dramatically around age 30, and it's clear that the simplistic imagery aimed for a particular effect that eventually became his signature style. For me, the surreal and simplified images guide the focus of the viewer from objective concrete details into subjective emotion. Indeed, had the female figure on the shore in "Separation" looked realistic, I'm certain it would have failed to get my attention. Instead of being allowed to observe the distracting details of the world, you are led to fill in the gaps with your own experience. And human figures that are clearly drawn as unrecognizable are more readily identified as ourselves or the other key players in our personal narratives.

Edvard Munch never married. Romantic heartache featured predominantly in his paintings. He said marriage wasn't conducive to his artistic lifestyle. I'm sure that pacified those who asked. I wonder if his rebuke of marriage was a front for his pain. If his decision was indeed conscious and as intentional as he made it sound, it is clear to me through his art that he processed pangs of regret or at least loss. His willingness to paint his own vulnerability distinguished him among the artists I admire. I've ruminated on whether he extended the same level of vulnerability in life.

I began a love affair with Munch's collection and reached the conclusion that a deeper appreciation for Munch's paintings could have value for more than just myself. Not only did Munch's art become a large component of this journal project, but the paintings also inspired me to create a relationship-themed tarot deck featuring his art.

For updates about other projects featuring Munch's work, visit:

www.redorchidpublishing.com

How to Use This Journal

There is no right or wrong way to use this journal. It is yours. But I will offer a few pro tips:

1- Cut out the "bookmarks" in the back of the journal. This is so you can lay the spread on the table and look at it without needing to weigh the sides of the book down and keep it open while reading. The backside of each bookmark is a brief reference for how to interpret more difficult questions from the accompanying spread. These charts are not intended to be used as full interpretations (they are too short for that) but should offer brief guidance on where to begin interpreting the card for that particular question.

2- It is not necessary to complete the journal linearly from page 1-52. You can choose the sections that speak to you and work through those first, and perhaps some not at all. You can repeat sections by adding notes in the reflection pages. Some sections you may not feel ready for. This is your journey, and the book was designed to cover possible needs, not provide compounding coursework.

3- This journal is not a thorough reference guide for card interpretation, and I encourage you to use either the literature your deck came with or online sources for interpretations. I do provide brief interpretation charts, but only as a bonus feature to be used in collaboration with your other references. It's best to use the charts when standard interpreation is elusive. This is primarily a journal.

4- This journal is designed to work with any tarot deck. You can even use a deck of regular poker playing cards (you just won't have major arcana cards to draw from)
Cups = Hearts, Swords = Spades, Pentacles = Clovers, Wands = Diamonds, and **Jacks** can be read as either **Pages** or **Knights**.

5- This journal is not intended to replace professional mental health services, counseling, or psychiatric medications.

6- It is ok to cry.

7- It is ok to not cry (you are still doing the work).

8- It is your spiritual birthright to heal emotionally; healing will come.

This book was created with sincere intent to facilitate healing, self-love, and growth. May you be blessed with self-awareness, insight, breakthroughs, and limitless strength on your healing journey. You are not alone.

Melanny

Color Chart

The Color Chart below is to be used for coloring the mandalas within each section. You can select colors from the chart before you begin, or you can color the mandala first, then return to this chart to unveil truths i the subconscious. Color choice should offer insight into what you are needing at the moment.

Color Interpretation

- Loyalty
- Trust
- Freedom
- Spirit
- Faith
- Affection
- Safety
- Kindness
- Harmony
- Joy
- Optimism
- Creativity

- Inner knowing
- Self-esteem
- Freedom
- Resilience
- Passion
- Innocence
- Daring
- Strength
- Nurturing
- Retreat
- Prayer
- Surrender

CHASE THE DRAGON

I've wandered this maze of the mind
three years and three months
slayed every beast
roaming the labyrinth,
aside from you.

I piled the rotting corpses in a corner,
and sent it ablaze;
easy work; their deaths exquisite
smoky shrines of justice.

The stench of the fires has faded.
I wander the stone path
anxious of its shadows,
and its, evil little memories;
I repeat over and over:
"I am alone, I am alone, I am alone."

You are the only survivor;
You are too quick for me,
darting around corners
when I'm not sure I've glimpsed you,
haunting me from out of reach.
But even when I had my chance,
I didn't strike,
just gazed at the scales of your back,
and strained to hear your dragon breath.

I really should finish you,

The scars you left are no more pleasant
than the scars by the others;
the terrors are gone now,
and the beauty and kindness
I carried in me,
that's gone too.

You wouldn't recognize this shattered,
walled-up woman
wanting nothing from you;
you'd trip over phantom branches,
with your clumsy hind legs,
gaze into the eyes of a stranger,
then grieve your sweetheart;
and irony with its hollow breastplate
would cast gongs into the night.

I keep leaving you dead vermin,
and I know I should stop.

There is no taming you,
or keeping you,
or feeding you.
There is only a small package
in bloody brown paper
lying in the road

the rotting love we squandered,

I suppose you will eat it.

–Melanny Eva Henson

Artwork: "Despair" 1893
Edvard Munch

What I believe about why he/she left:

Who they were to me:

Who I was to them:

What I really deserve:

If there's one thing I continue to believe about this situation that is untrue, it is:

Deep down, I know that

You left...

"Not belonging is a terrible feeling. It feels awkward and it hurts, as if you were wearing someone else's shoes."

-Phoebe Stone

You will miss me because

You really hurt me when you

I feel so alone

My heart hurts

If I saw you again, I would say

COLOR ME

Mantra: I deserve love

Reflections

*"Melancholy" 1910
Edvard Munch*

BETRAYAL

"The Murderess" 1906
Edvard Munch

CONVERSATION WITH THE HUNTSMAN

Tears flowed in waves
I tried to cast a morning
like other mornings;
buttered toast,
and the ambivalent tone
of newscasters speaking
distant horrors.

"We must let this dark memory die
of natural causes," I say.
For now, we gently discuss
pulling the plug;
we scrape eggs across fine china,
drowning the cries of this ghost.

You understand.

I exhale relief with the faint burn
of tobasco.
We share a pat of butter alongside
the comfort of extended metaphor.
You say I had been Snow White,
and you The Huntsman.

We set a place at the table
for that dark truth,
for ill intentions, contrasted so nicely
against affection and jam,
against my safe heart beating
beneath broken ribs.

Truth sat there awkwardly,
our third wheel, eavesdropping,
hogging the coffee creamer.

You rose, and drew the curtains,
hoping I wouldn't notice the rain,
but I've grown accustomed
to these storms.

I can only breathe
when the lightning's on me,
when I can spot something
in the darkness to fight,
and when the sun comes out,
I listen for the thunder.

Rain is what I know.

Set down your breakfast fork,
take my pale hand;
I'll guide you back to that place
in the woods,
show you how much sweeter
the apples are here,
demonstrate the weakness
of your blade on the tip
of my immortal finger,

"Hold my hand a little tighter, darling.
It will be a good death."

–Melanny Eva Henson

Artwork: "Murder in the Lane" 1919
Edvard Munch

I believe you betrayed me because

I still don't understand   This betrayal changed me by   I still think about

This is what needs to heal within me:

This is what I need in order to heal:

13

You betrayed me...

"If you're betrayed, release disappointment at once. By that way, the bitterness has no time to take root."

-Toba Beta

Things might have been different, but they may not have been better because

I deserved better because

I feel empty

"You are going to break your promise. I understand. And I hold my hands over the ears of my heart, so that I will not hate you."

-Catherynne M. Valente

I'll be fine without you, but I would have preferred to be fine with you because

COLOR ME

Mantra: I deserve loyalty

REFLECTIONS

"The Murderer" 1910
Edvard Munch

"Anxiety" 1894
Edvard Munch

THE AWKWARD ART OF FORGIVENESS

I can't seem to master the strokes;
the brush trembles in my fingers.
Maybe an apology would spark the muse,
but they all tell me it won't.

This canvas is messy, obstructed, melting.
I can't concentrate over the high-pitched
whine of my heart, a kettle steaming.
Some days, there's nothing
but peaceful lake views,
and fall leaves, and the gentle
muffles of a sleeping puppy;

But other days, there's you.
You, and then the version of me you painted;
a grotesque image I can't stop studying,
comparing the likeness;
my heart drops into some deep well,
as a child's cry echoes from its depths.

I think I've destroyed your painting,
torched it angrily, tossed it out
carelessly, buried it lovingly;
it returns, the cursed Ouija board,
just as I'm sure it's gone.
I can't seem to create my own
painting without remembering yours,
allowing its falseness to creep up my arm,
into the itch of my fingers,
growing vines of disturbed lies.

I'm digging in the yard of my mind
for the right emotion, the right thought,
the right attitude;

There are holes across this landscape
beside piles of dirt.

I say, "I forgive you.
I forgive you. I forgive you."
I say it like a recited prayer,
I chastise myself for my clumsy forgiveness,
my sharp memory, my broken heart.

This is embarrassing.

I paint myself in white drapes,
read the words of others
who have transcended this space;
I form this woman honest and whole.

But then, I feel I must paint her a cane,
lest she spend eternity hobbling in agony.
I stop upon the lame truth,
let the paint dry over
this weak leg of isolation.

Her sad eyes reach into the room
as the late hour beckons me to bed.
Before dropping the heavy brush
into the baptismal font
of a plastic red cup,
I paint your thin hand in the corner:

disembodied,
open,

reaching for me.

–Melanny Eva Henson

ARTWORK: "THE HANDS" 1893
EDVARD MUNCH

I think my anxiety started when

My fear(s)

My trigger(s)

The root of my anxiety

I can calm my fears by

I can manage my triggers by

I can uproot my anxiety by

I'm afraid...

"Whatever happens to you belongs to you. Make it yours. Feed it to yourself even if it feels impossible to swallow. Let it nurture you because it will."

-Cheryl Strayed

I worry about

I can't stop thinking about

"Tension is who you think you should be. Relaxation is who you are."

-Chinese Proverb

will I be ok?

"You have dug your soul out of the dark, you have fought to be here; do not go back to what buried you."

-Bianca Sparacino

When I look to the future, I feel

COLOR ME

Mantra: I am enough

Reflections

"The Scream" 1893
Edvard Munch

IDENTITY

"Nude in Front of a Mirror" 1917

Edvard Munch

WE WERE ALWAYS QUEENS

We were always queens,
even in the swallows of poverty,
tasting snow in our thin coats,
our tongues rubbing the holes
of broken teeth
we couldn't afford to replace;
even in the neighborhood
where the ceiling had stains,
and we slept behind doors with picked locks.

We were always queens,
even when the boys called us ugly,
and the teacher said we didn't do it right;
even when our mother screamed at us for
leaving the fridge open
for ruining our food
for needing her to fill our bellies
when no one would fill hers,
and the homework lie blank in a bag,
taunting us with all the things we weren't
and had not done.

We were always queens,
even when the pastor showed us
how good wives hold it together,
how to hold the needle and stitch
the wounds into cloth,
three shades of bright red to drape over
whatever lay dead in us;
even when the milk ran out,
and we couldn't find the strength
to return from the store.

We were always queens,
even when our minds were heavy with defeat,
when we felt safer in darkness,
hiding from the world
and its constant rejection,
when we cast the love that no one wanted
into the shadows,
and shed thirsty tears
into the cup of regret.

We were always queens,
even when our true loves betrayed us,
left us with the Rubik's cube
of a table for one;
even as we sat in our fat,
marinating in self loathing
gazing with muted bitterness
at a world that refused to see us;

as we sighed between sips of soda
as the inner lights dimmed,
as the curtain called,
yes, even then,
we were queens.

-Melanny Eva Henson

ARTWORK: "WOMAN WITH POPPIES" 1919
EDVARD MUNCH

I've lost the part of me that

Who I know I am

Who I am beneath the surface

The part of me I'm still searching for

Who I am becoming:

I am ...

Who I used to be

"Human beings are not born once and for all on the day their mothers give birth to them, but life obliges them over and over again to give birth to themselves."

— Gabriel García Márquez

The person I am now

"When I discover who I am, I'll be free."

-Ralph Ellison

where have I gone?

The person I want to be

"I belong to the people I love, and they belong to me--they, and the love and loyalty I give them, form my identity far more than any word or group ever could."

-Veronica Roth

COLOR ME

Mantra: I am

REFLECTIONS

"Nude in front of a Mirror" *1902*
Edvard Munch

DESPAIR

"Ashes" 1894
Edvard Munch

WHEN THEY BREAK YOU

When they break you, don't be afraid.
Those tiny fractures let the light in.
Don't fear your own brokenness,
or think that your scattered pieces
mean you are not whole.

You are whole like the rivers and lakes
finding each other.
You are whole like the separate continents,
you are whole like the tiny cells within you,
dividing as they die.

So there are pieces.
Don't listen as the others point,
as they walk away.
These pieces can build
the safety of a castle,
or steps up the mountain,
or form a great ship to cross the sea.

You are not these pieces.
You are the master of them.
You mustn't let anyone convince you
to sell them for scrap,
or pile them in a box
to store in the attic.

People will fear your brokenness,
but you should not.
Too many fear their own brokenness
and enter that ocean of slavery.
There's a current of fear,
and it feels natural to swim with it;
it feels almost right.

They will push you into that current
and in the next breath,
they will point out that you
have been swept away,
that you won't ever find your feet.

But you will.
They are in the next turn,
near the shore,
you can pull yourself from the water,
gather up your diamonds
in the hem of your shirt,

and walk.

–Melanny Eva Henson

ARTWORK: "CONSOLATION IN THE FOREST" 1924
EDVARD MUNCH

I struggle to

At the heart of
my despair

What I know I'm
grieving over

What I'm too afraid
to look at

What I need to heal:

I lost you ...

"Only people who are capable of loving strongly can also suffer great sorrow, but this same necessity of loving serves to counteract their grief and heals them."

— Leo Tolstoy

I grieve for

I always think about

what will life look like without you?

I struggle to move forward because

"I will not say: do not weep; for not all tears are an evil."

-J.R.R. Tolkien

REFLECTIONS

"The Sick Child" 1885
Edvard Munch

BARGAINING

"Cupid and Psyche" 1907
Edvard Munch

THE BLACK TREES

I won't make you sorry
with lightning success
or an angry, well versed letter;
or pique your sorrow
with a barrage of joyful photos
frozen to perfection.

Instead, I'll fetter the talons of regret
through three deep breaths
at sunrise,
gaze at the cardinal
dipping a Birch branch
outside my window.
I'll stir a quaint spoon
in torrid coffee,
and as the creamer swirls
like marbled paint,
within a dark maelstrom,
I'll know that I am me.

I wandered the mountains
of our landscape
formed from each breadcrumb text.
I've mapped those hills
searching for your glorious view;

you've led me through
the thickets of Narcissus.

My phantom tears gather
in the shadow cloud of indifference
and condense into a mending rain.
These beads of brood
weep through our ozone
of collective conscience,
a heat seeking missile of justice;

guilt rings
in your stubborn left ear,
half dumb to me, yet half listening
for the dreadful judgment
of my voice.

In the deep canyons
of our dark planet,
I stop shredding my arms
on your thorned branches,
and the mountains open their jaws;

the cardinal song pops the air,
the coffee hot and rich,
and I close my eyes,
gloriously deaf
to your voice beckoning
through the black trees.

–Melanny Eva Henson

Artwork: "autumn" 1919
Edvard Munch

What I had that is now gone

What I want

What I think I did wrong

The desire driving my thoughts

The truth about what I did or didn't do

How I will get what I need or want

If only...

"Every broken heart has screamed at one time or another: Why can't you see who I truly am?"

-Shannon L. Alder

In my mind, I keep replaying

I wish I had

I should have...

I'm struggling to accept

"Another form of bargaining, and she did it too, is to replay the final painful moments over and over in her head as if by doing so she could eventually create a different outcome. It is natural to replay in your mind the details. Deep in your heart, you know what is true. You go over and over and over it in your mind. Your heart replays the scene for you for the express purpose of teaching you to accept what has happened."

-Kate McGahan, Jack McAfghan

COLOR ME

Mantra: I am truth

REFLECTIONS

"Under the Stars" *1900*
Edvard Munch

UNREQUITED LOVE

"The Lonely Ones" 1896
Edvard Munch

ME ESCAPING YOU

This is the price:

The nothing,
the silence,
the abyss of radio squelch,
flashing red text,
and the incessant ding
of a car door.

You disintegrate into this absence,
only the ghost of memories
for company;
distracting flies
you swat at
between swigs.

This knowing rattles within you,
this break in the soul
has become your familiar;
a ragged cough,
a torn, stained sofa
you can't afford to replace.

You mourn,
but it's a secret mourning,
tucked in the shadows
of your heart;
and you cried once
as you walked alone
near the end of a dark rain.

Mostly, the tears run
down other faces,
in some other chasm
between earth and ether,

I wander there,
blind, arms out for the path,
pressing to escape through
a sigh,
a breath,
a laugh.

—Melanny Eva Henson

Artwork: "the lonely ones" 1935
Edvard Munch

Why we are no longer together

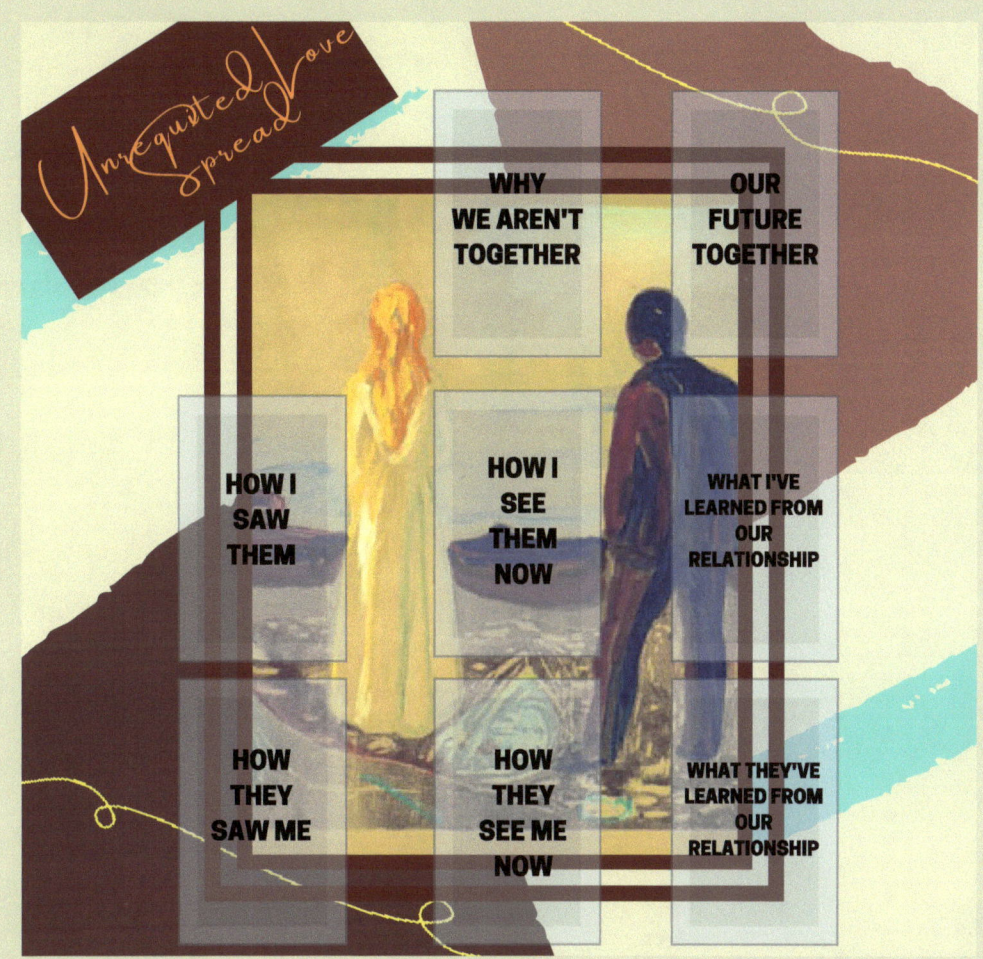

Our future together:

How I saw them

How I see them now

What I've learned from our relationship

How they saw me

How they see me now

What they've learned from our relationship

You didn't love me

"Love Jo all your days, if you choose, but don't let it spoil you, for it's wicked to throw away so many good gifts because you can't have the one you want."

-Louisa May Alcott

If you had loved me, you would have

I loved you because

I deserved more

"I had to get over [him]. For months now, a stone had been sitting on my heart. I'd shed a lot of tears over [him], lost a lot of sleep, eaten a lot of cake batter. Somehow, I had to move on. [Life] would be hell if I didn't shake loose from the grip he had on my heart. I most definitely didn't want to keep feeling this way, alone in a love affair meant for two. Even if he'd felt like The One. Even if I'd always thought we'd end up together. Even if he still had a choke chain on my heart."

-Kristan Higgins

I forgive myself for loving you because

COLOR ME

Mantra: I give and receive love

Reflections

"Weeping Nude" 1913
Edvard Munch

HEALING

"The Sun" 1910
Edvard Munch

RED PHOENIX

When I wake,
a tune vanishes,
black wings fluttering.
I open my eyes
to stripes of light
from the blinds,
the lucid notes evaporate
into ceiling tiles
and rumblings
of the morning garbage truck.

In the tender bite of November air,
with my wings folded neatly
beneath my red coat,
I ask the trees about these dreams,
about the songs drifting from me.
They say I can heal now,
and my joy will give birth
to my capacity for more pain.

You will pass through me, finally,
like a stubborn kidney stone,
they said.

I am vicious with my happiness,
vindicated for all the tears I gathered,
sent overnight delivery,
and when you rejected them,
wouldn't even open the package,
I cried more.

half my heart burst into red flame,
coiled with smoke,
while you sat on your gray couch
snapping Doritos,
the sparks of your empty laughter
drowning the crude joy of
Saturday Night Live,
and all that you refused to do
neatly buried in a drawer.

I don't recall the songs,
Those unconscious melodies of balm,
but I remember the confusion,
the awkwardness of non-closure,
the half-told joke,
the half-letter,
the half-conversation,
dreaming half-woman, half monster-ape,
half brilliance, yet half worthless,
and only a half mirror
showing me my horror.

The nightmares are fading now
into faint emotions going in and out,
like an old camera lens never focusing.

I've stopped taking pictures.

I've learned to take the scenery in while I can,
let the trees enter me without distraction,
and the stone moves.
Within the nest of my warm coat
I think I might feel
the faint tapping of the phoenix beak
beneath my rib.

–Melanny Eva Henson

ARTWORK: "WOMAN IN A RED DRESS" 1902
EDVARD MUNCH

The pain of the past

What I know I need   What I'm battling   How the spirt world
in order to heal   subconscioiusly   will help me

How I will know I have healed:

I'm healing

""If you desire healing,
let yourself fall ill
let yourself fall ill."

—Rumi

I will start to heal when

My best coping strategy is

"The wound is the place where the Light enters you."

—Rumi

I will know I've healed when

""Wounding and healing are not opposites. They're part of the same thing. It is our wounds that enable us to be compassionate with the wounds of others. It is our limitations that make us kind to the limitations of other people. It is our loneliness that helps us to to find other people or to even know they're alone with an illness. I think I have served people perfectly with parts of myself I used to be ashamed of."

—Rachel Naomi Remen

COLOR ME

MANTRA: I AM WHOLE

REFLECTIONS

"The Sun" 1910
Edvard Munch

53

THE KARMA OWED TO ME

0-Fool New beginning	I-Magician Personal power	II-High Priestess Intuitive Guidance	III-Empress Children	IV-Emperor Self-mastery	V-Hierophant Wedding
VI- Lovers A great love	VII-Chariot A journey	VIII- Justice Justice to be served	IX- Hermit Isolation for growth	X-Wheel of Fortune Good luck	XI- Strength healing
XII- Hanged Man A break	XIII- Death A major life change	XIV- Temperance Balance	XV- Devil Power	XVI- Tower A do-over	XVII- Star A sign
XVIII- Moon Guidance in dreams	XX- Sun Joy	XX- Judgment Reckoning	XI- World Public Knowledge	Ace of Swords The truth	2 of Swords Blind to toxicity
3 of Swords Who hurt you will hurt	4 of Swords A retreat	5 of Swords Enemy will be defeated	6 of Swords Travels	7 of Swords Betrayer will be betrayed	8 of Swords Self-perception will heal
9 of Swords Cognitive therapy	10 of Swords An end to suffering	Page of Swords A messenger	Knight of Swords Courage	Queen of Swords A connection severed	King of Swords Education
Ace of Cups Love	2 of Cups Commitment	3 of Cups Friendship	4 of Cups Abuser is unhappy	5 of Cups Abuser feels the loss	6 of Cups Family loyalty
7 of Cups Opportunities	8 of Cups Finding something better	9 of Cups Wish granted	10 of Cups Fulfillment	Page of Cups An apology	Knight of Cups A proposal
Queen of Cups A trustworthy woman	King of Cups A kind man	Ace of Wands Inspiration	2 of Wands A solid plan	3 of Wands Return on investment	4 of Wands A stable home
5 of Wands An end to conflict	6 of Wands A victory	7 of Wands Can beat the enemy	8 of Wands A message is coming	9 of Wands Finding your way out	10 of Wands Able to manage stress
Page of Wands An attainable goal	Knight of Wands Drive	Queen of Wands Visual talent	King of Wands Leadership talent	Ace of Pentacles Money	2 of Pentacles A good change
3 of Pentacles A good team	4 of Pentacles Savings	5 of Pentacles Survival	6 of Pentacles Charity/help	7 of Pentacles Harvest	8 of Pentacles Opportunity to advance
9 of Pentacles Independence	10 of Pentacles Family security	Page of Pentacles Project idea	Knight of Pentacles someone you need stays	Queen of Pentacles Nurturing woman	King of Pentacles Reliable man

WHAT I NEED IN ORDER TO HEAL

0-Fool New beginnings	I-Magician Personal power	II-High Priestess Intuition	III-Empress Divine feminine	IV-Emperor Self-mastery	V-Hierophant Tradition/ritual
VI- Lovers Major decision	VII-Chariot Make a choice	VIII- Justice Justice to be served	IX- Hermit Meditation	X-Wheel of Fortune Healing comes	XI- Strength Reflect on your wound
XII- Hanged Man Time	XIII- Death A major life change	XIV- Temperance Daily routine	XV- Devil Take control	XVI- Tower Destroy the enemy's hold	XVII- Star Spiritual message
XVIII- Moon Dream therapy	XX- Sun More joy	XX- Judgment Clarity	XI- World Coming out with your truth	Ace of Swords Tell the truth	2 of Swords Look past others' faults
3 of Swords Tend to your wounds	4 of Swords Rest	5 of Swords Defeat your fear	6 of Swords Travel or move on	7 of Swords Put yourself first	8 of Swords Change self
9 of Swords Cognitive therapy	10 of Swords Pick yourself up	Page of Swords Write letter you don't send	night of Swords Courage	Queen of Swords Cut off your abuser	King of Swords Strategy
Ace of Cups Love	2 of Cups Commitment	3 of Cups Friendship	4 of Cups Find your passion	5 of Cups Count blessings	6 of Cups Family
7 of Cups Create options	8 of Cups Walk away	9 of Cups Believe in miracles	10 of Cups Find what fulfills you	Page of Cups Extend love to others	Knight of Cups Donate to others
Queen of Cups Heal the mother	King of Cups Heal the father	Ace of Wands Pursue your passion	2 of Wands Plan a change	3 of Wands Deal with a third party	4 of Wands Stability
5 of Wands Stop arguing	6 of Wands Small victories	7 of Wands Know your worth	8 of Wands Communication	9 of Wands Find the door out	10 of Wands Eliminate the stressors
Page of Wands Set a goal	Knight of Wands Pursue your goal	Queen of Wands Talk to others	King of Wands Create art	Ace of Pentacles Put down roots	2 of Pentacles Find balance
3 of Pentacles Couple/family therapy	4 of Pentacles Budget	5 of Pentacles Financial security	6 of Pentacles Listen to others'	7 of Pentacles Plant seeds of change	8 of Pentacles Apprenticeship
9 of Pentacles Independence	10 of Pentacles Family security	Page of Pentacles Project	Knight of Pentacles Commit to one place	Queen of Pentacles Nurture children	King of Pentacles Be dependable

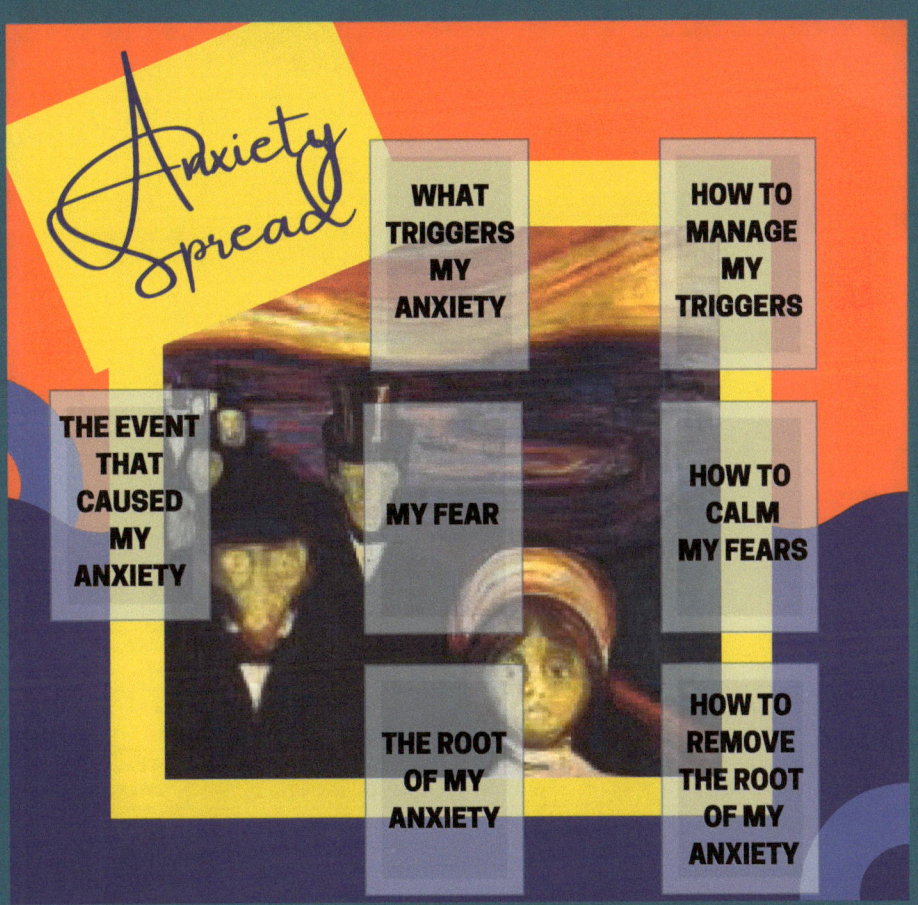

HOW TO REMOVE MY ANXIETY

0-Fool New beginning	I-Magician Find a resource	II-High Priestess Watch and wait	III-Empress Create	IV-Emperor Manage environment	V-Hierophant Follow tradition
VI- Lovers Make a choice	VII-Chariot Find direction	VIII- Justice Be fair to yourself	IX- Hermit Meditation	X-Wheel of Fortune Fate will help	XI- Strength Tend the wound
XII- Hanged Man Withdraw for a bit	XIII- Death A major life change	XIV- Temperance Establish routine	XV- Devil Take control	XVI- Tower End this	XVII- Star Follow your gut
XVIII- Moon Listen to your guides	XX- Sun Find joy/ join society	XX- Judgment Finally see the truth	XI- World Public declaration	Ace of Swords Write your truth	2 of Swords Ignore racing thoughts
3 of Swords Acknowledge heartbreak	4 of Swords Sleep/rest	5 of Swords Face your enemy	6 of Swords Move on to better	7 of Swords Take your life back	8 of Swords See the real you
9 of Swords Cognitive therapy	10 of Swords One step at a time	Page of Swords Write a plan	Knight of Swords Confront the problem	Queen of Swords Sever a connection	King of Swords Write down goals
Ace of Cups Remember your light	2 of Cups Commit	3 of Cups Socialize more	4 of Cups Don't decide just yet	5 of Cups Count your blessings	6 of Cups Nostalgia
7 of Cups Create choices	8 of Cups Find something better	9 of Cups Dream big	10 of Cups Music or painting	Page of Cups Donate time	Knight of Cups Help others
Queen of Cups Focus on love	King of Cups Be kind to yourself	Ace of Wands Chase inspiration	2 of Wands Set goals and steps	3 of Wands Wait for returns	4 of Wands Build a stable home
5 of Wands Confront the conflict	6 of Wands You need a win	7 of Wands Know your worth	8 of Wands Communication	9 of Wands Find your way out	10 of Wands Manage stress
Page of Wands Take steps towards goal	Knight of Wands Pursue goals intensely	Queen of Wands Create beauty	King of Wands Create art	Ace of Pentacles Know what grounds you	2 of Pentacles Swap something
3 of Pentacles Collaboration	4 of Pentacles Save time/resources	5 of Pentacles Let go of possessions	6 of Pentacles Charity/help others	7 of Pentacles Just wait—it gets better	8 of Pentacles Career goals
9 of Pentacles Independence	10 of Pentacles Family security	Page of Pentacles Project idea in action	Knight of Pentacles Make a firm decision	Queen of Pentacles Find stability	King of Pentacles Manage finances

WHO I AM / IDENTITY

0-Fool Adventurer	I-Magician Magical person	II-High Priestess Intuitive	III- Empress Creator	IV-Emperor Powerful	V-Hierophant Traditional
VI- Lovers Romantic	VII-Chariot Incredibly driven	VIII- Justice Value fairness	IX- Hermit Wise	X-Wheel of Fortune You trust fate	XI- Strength A healer
XII- Hanged Man You know when to quit	XIII- Death You offer perspective	XIV- Temperance You are predictable	XV- Devil You put yourself first	XVI- Tower You call out falseness	XVII- Star You guide others
XVIII- Moon You are psychic	XX- Sun You are fun	XX- Judgment You see through people	XI- World You are popular/famous	Ace of Swords You are honest	2 of Swords You ignore faults
3 of Swords Identity is through your pain	4 of Swords You don't overwork	5 of Swords High conflict	6 of Swords Search for peace	7 of Swords Clever	8 of Swords You see through obscurity
9 of Swords Dreams tell future	10 of Swords You know how to survive	Page of Swords A writer	Knight of Swords Hot-headed	Queen of Swords Know when to say no	King of Swords A strategist
Ace of Cups Full of love	2 of Cups Committed	3 of Cups Social	4 of Cups Not impulsive	5 of Cups Sensitive	6 of Cups Value family
7 of Cups Vivid fantasies	8 of Cups You know what you deserve	9 of Cups Lucky	10 of Cups Emotionally stable	Page of Cups Fun-loving	Knight of Cups Heroic
Queen of Cups Loving	King of Cups Kind	Ace of Wands Full of inspiration	2 of Wands A planner	3 of Wands Good investor	4 of Wands Reliable
5 of Wands Confrontational	6 of Wands Prone to success	7 of Wands A champion	8 of Wands Communicator	9 of Wands Escapes consequences	10 of Wands Prone to depression
Page of Wands Creative but no focus	Knight of Wands Goal-oriented	Queen of Wands Physically attractive	King of Wands Creative with focus	Ace of Pentacles Resourceful / A resource	2 of Pentacles Duplicitous
3 of Pentacles A team player	4 of Pentacles A saver	5 of Pentacles Poverty mentality	6 of Pentacles Charitable	7 of Pentacles Patient	8 of Pentacles Career oriented
9 of Pentacles Independent	10 of Pentacles Strong family / roots	Page of Pentacles Project oriented	Knight of Pentacles Dependable	Queen of Pentacles Motherly	King of Pentacles Rich

WHAT I AM GRIEVING OVER

0-Fool Your innocence	I-Magician Your personal power	II-High Priestess Your connection to Spirit	III- Empress Mother	IV-Emperor Father	V-Hierophant Tradition
VI- Lovers A great love	VII-Chariot Loss of drive	VIII- Justice Injustice	IX- Hermit Cut off from society	X-Wheel of Fortune Bad luck	XI- Strength A deep wound
XII- Hanged Man No closure	XIII- Death A permanent change	XIV- Temperance Loss of balance	XV- Devil Addictions	XVI- Tower An accident	XVII- Star No path forward
XVIII- Moon No insight / Deception	XX- Sun No joy	XX- Judgment What you understand now	XI- World Public image	Ace of Swords A hurtful truth	2 of Swords What you didn't see
3 of Swords A crushing blow	4 of Swords Illness or death	5 of Swords A bad fight/physical	6 of Swords What you left behind	7 of Swords What was stolen from you	8 of Swords What you can't see clearly
9 of Swords Trauma	10 of Swords A bitter and difficult end	Page of Swords A communicative friend	Knight of Swords Hot-headed male	Queen of Swords A vicious woman	King of Swords A manipulator
Ace of Cups Lost potential	2 of Cups A broken agreement	3 of Cups Social ties severed	4 of Cups No good options	5 of Cups A great loss	6 of Cups Lost childhood
7 of Cups A fantasy unrealized	8 of Cups What you left behind	9 of Cups Still wishing	10 of Cups Lack of fulfillment	Page of Cups Loving friend	Knight of Cups A romantic
Queen of Cups Loving woman	King of Cups Kind man	Ace of Wands Lack of inspiration	2 of Wands No solid plans	3 of Wands Bad investment	4 of Wands Instability
5 of Wands Confrontation	6 of Wands Lack of success	7 of Wands Fighting too long	8 of Wands Lack of communication	9 of Wands Stuck	10 of Wands Overwhelmed
Page of Wands Creative friend	Knight of Wands Goal-oriented person	Queen of Wands Creative woman	King of Wands Creative man	Ace of Pentacles Lack of resources	2 of Pentacles A bad change
3 of Pentacles Lack of teamwork	4 of Pentacles Control	5 of Pentacles Loss of money	6 of Pentacles Can't help others	7 of Pentacles Waited too long	8 of Pentacles Lacking career
9 of Pentacles Dependency	10 of Pentacles Loss of family ties	Page of Pentacles Dedicated friend	Knight of Pentacles Unfortunate arrival	Queen of Pentacles Resourceful woman	King of Pentacles Resourceful man

THE TRUTH ABOUT WHAT I DID OR DIDN'T DO

0-Fool You are innocent	I-Magician You are powerful	II-High Priestess You have spiritual authority	III- Empress You create	IV-Emperor You are in charge	V-Hierophant Tradition is why
VI- Lovers Someone made a choice	VII-Chariot You steer the ship	VIII- Justice Justice will prevail	IX- Hermit You are wiser than you think	X-Wheel of Fortune Fate is in control	XI- Strength This is a path to healing
XII- Hanged Man You couldn't have stopped it	XIII- Death This is permanent	XIV- Temperance You are balanced	XV- Devil Blame addiction/vices	XVI- Tower Environment is why	XVII- Star You will know
XVIII- Moon You don't have all the facts	XX- Sun Joy is yours	XX- Judgment You need clarity	XI- World Information is public	Ace of Swords A hurtful truth	2 of Swords What you didn't see
3 of Swords Your heart still hurts	4 of Swords You need rest	5 of Swords Can't trust this person	6 of Swords It will get better	7 of Swords There's a thief involved	8 of Swords Change your thinking
9 of Swords Dreams have answers	10 of Swords A bitter and difficult end	Page of Swords Need documentation	Knight of Swords They like fighting	Queen of Swords You need to break ties	King of Swords You need a strategy
Ace of Cups There is hope	2 of Cups A have commitment	3 of Cups You have friends	4 of Cups You don't like your options	5 of Cups Struggle to get over it	6 of Cups Connected to the past
7 of Cups Your head's in the clouds	8 of Cups You should move on	9 of Cups A wish will be granted	10 of Cups You need fulfillment	Page of Cups Need empathy	Knight of Cups You crave romance
Queen of Cups You're a good person	King of Cups Kindness will save you	Ace of Wands Don't forget your fire	2 of Wands You need a plan	3 of Wands Expect a return	4 of Wands You can rebuild
5 of Wands Conflict of interests	6 of Wands You will succeed	7 of Wands You have the upper hand	8 of Wands Expect communication	9 of Wands Get unstuck	10 of Wands Too many commitments
Page of Wands Need passion	Knight of Wands You need drive	Queen of Wands Create beauty	King of Wands Lead by example	Ace of Pentacles You have resources	2 of Pentacles Swap something
3 of Pentacles You can rely on others	4 of Pentacles Someone is withholding	5 of Pentacles Focus on Spirit	6 of Pentacles Someone will help you	7 of Pentacles Need patience	8 of Pentacles Need career goals
9 of Pentacles All you need is you	10 of Pentacles Rely on family	Page of Pentacles Need the tangible	Knight of Pentacles Need dependability	Queen of Pentacles You are resourceful	King of Pentacles You will find wealth

HOW SOMEONE IS SEEN

0-Fool Innocent or foolish	I-Magician Magical/powerful	II-High Priestess Spiritually authoritative	III- Empress Sexy/fertile	IV-Emperor Worldly/powerful	V-Hierophant Traditional
VI- Lovers A soul mate	VII-Chariot Driven	VIII- Justice Fair	IX- Hermit Quiet	X-Wheel of Fortune Free spirited	XI- Strength Strong or wounded or both
XII- Hanged Man Uninvolved	XIII- Death Inspires you to change	XIV- Temperance Balanced	XV- Devil Addicting or toxic	XVI- Tower Destructive	XVII- Star Spiritual
XVIII- Moon Secretive	XX- Sun Joyful	XX- Judgment Good judgment	XI- World Popular	Ace of Swords Truthful	2 of Swords Blind
3 of Swords Hurt	4 of Swords Grieving	5 of Swords Violent / vicious	6 of Swords In transition	7 of Swords Deceptive/dishonest	8 of Swords Overly humble
9 of Swords Anxious	10 of Swords Coming out of difficulty	Page of Swords Articulate	Knight of Swords Aggressive	Queen of Swords Formidable / winter	King of Swords Cold / educated
Ace of Cups Loving	2 of Cups Committed	3 of Cups Social	4 of Cups Discontent	5 of Cups Pessimistic	6 of Cups Nostalgic
7 of Cups A big dreamer	8 of Cups Fed up	9 of Cups Faithful	10 of Cups Happy	Page of Cups Empathetic	Knight of Cups Romantic
Queen of Cups Gracious	King of Cups Good with people	Ace of Wands Has good ideas	2 of Wands A good planner	3 of Wands A good investor	4 of Wands Stable
5 of Wands Argumentative	6 of Wands A winner	7 of Wands A good fighter	8 of Wands Good communicator	9 of Wands A martyr	10 of Wands Depressed
Page of Wands Visionary	Knight of Wands Undeterred	Queen of Wands Lovely	King of Wands Inspirational	Ace of Pentacles Resourceful	2 of Pentacles Shifty
3 of Pentacles Good with people	4 of Pentacles Conservative or controlling	5 of Pentacles Poor	6 of Pentacles Charitable	7 of Pentacles Patient	8 of Pentacles Career oriented
9 of Pentacles Independent	10 of Pentacles Family oriented	Page of Pentacles Project oriented	Knight of Pentacles Fixed, unmoving	Queen of Pentacles Has everything	King of Pentacles Wealthy

HOW THE SPIRIT WORLD WILL HELP ME

0-Fool Create new beginning	I-Magician Help with magic	II-High Priestess Intuitive Knowing	III- Empress Fertility	IV-Emperor Virility	V-Hierophant Traditional spirits will guide
VI- Lovers Bring you a soul mate	VII-Chariot Bring you an impasse	VIII- Justice Deliver justice	IX- Hermit Talk to you in meditation	X-Wheel of Fortune Fated event coming	XI- Strength Help with healing
XII- Hanged Man Keep toxicity away	XIII- Death Bring a welcome change	XIV- Temperance Encourage your daily balance	XV- Devil Healing addiction	XVI- Tower Destroy what's in your way	XVII- Star Send signs
XVIII- Moon Full moon enlightenment	XX- Sun Joyful experience	XX- Judgment Bring karma	XI- World Many spirits are helping	Ace of Swords Help you see the truth	2 of Swords Help remove blinders
3 of Swords Remove emotional pain	4 of Swords Create chance to rest	5 of Swords Revenge your enemies	6 of Swords Calm the storm	7 of Swords Reveal deception	8 of Swords Help connect the real you
9 of Swords Alleviate anxiety	10 of Swords Help pick you up	Page of Swords Deliver messages	Knight of Swords Fight for you	Queen of Swords Cut off those not for you	King of Swords Put you in right place/time
Ace of Cups Fill you with love	2 of Cups Bring you a partner	3 of Cups Bring you friends	4 of Cups Help you find your way out	5 of Cups Comfort you	6 of Cups Past life memories
7 of Cups Bring you vivid visions	8 of Cups Help you walk away	9 of Cups Grant a wish	10 of Cups Rejoice with you	Page of Cups Deliver love message	Knight of Cups Bring romance
Queen of Cups Show you love	King of Cups Show you kindness	Ace of Wands Inspire you	2 of Wands Help you plan	3 of Wands Deliver rewards	4 of Wands Provide stability
5 of Wands Help resolve conflict	6 of Wands Bring a victory	7 of Wands Help you in a fight	8 of Wands Direct communication	9 of Wands An escape	10 of Wands Alleviate depression
Page of Wands Visions	Knight of Wands Help keep you driven	Queen of Wands Visual art assistance	King of Wands Direction with action	Ace of Pentacles Resources	2 of Pentacles Bring a good change
3 of Pentacles Bring a good team	4 of Pentacles Help you save money	5 of Pentacles Heal poverty	6 of Pentacles Bring you a gift	7 of Pentacles Grant patience	8 of Pentacles Career guidance
9 of Pentacles Financial guidance	10 of Pentacles Bring you family	Page of Pentacles Attainable project	Knight of Pentacles Companionship	Queen of Pentacles Nurture your soul	King of Pentacles Foster confidence

www.ingramcontent.com/pod-product-compliance
Lightning Source LLC
Chambersburg PA
CBHW042012150426
43195CB00003B/103